THE SILENT SYNDROME

THE SILENT SYNDROME

Cheryl Jost

Library of Congress Control Number:		2017917603
ISBN:	Hardcover	978-1-5434-6610-2
	Softcover	978-1-5434-6609-6
	eBook	978-1-5434-6806-9

Print information available on the last page.

Rev. date: 02/15/2018

To order additional copies of this book, contact:
Xlibris
1-888-795-4274
www.Xlibris.com
Orders@Xlibris.com
769259

CONTENTS

To my mother.

She was my strongest advocate, mentor, and supporter of my book. Her ultimate gift of love to me has given me the strength and courage to carry on without her by my side. Getting this book published was a lifetime dream of mine and she was instrumental in making it come true. I will be eternally grateful to her.

To my father.

Thanks for *always* being there for me. I love you more than words can say. You are the ultimate example of perfect love. God truly blessed me when he let me be born into this family.

To my brother and sisters.

Thanks for tolerating me and sharing my roller-coaster life! I'm so glad we have one another to lean on.

To my family and friends who gave me the inspiration to write this book. Without their devotion and unconditional love, I would not have been able to cope with living with Turner Syndrome. Thanks for putting up with me throughout the years!

CHAPTER 1

Introduction: Why I'm Writing This Book

I would like to share with you some of my personal views on what it's like to be diagnosed with Turner Syndrome and how you go about accepting it so that you can lead a normal and fulfilling life. It is a scary and shocking thing when you first hear the words "Your daughter has Turner Syndrome." But what does it really mean for your daughter? Most parents are petrified because of the unknown. You will find that education is the best tool against this virtually unknown, ostentatious-sounding syndrome. When I was diagnosed at the age of eleven in 1971, there was not much information available out there for my parents. Heck, the Internet wasn't even heard of yet. That is another reason for me writing this book—to help educate parents so that they can learn what to expect and how to best handle those delicate times they will have to face in the future as they raise their beautiful daughter.

It is also very important to educate the public and medical community to eliminate old stigmas and misinformation associated with Turner Syndrome because of outdated material in libraries and schools. One way I have tried to do this is by working very hard to educate the medical community. As past president of the Saint Louis Chapter of the Turner Syndrome Society of the United States, I was asked to visit a genetics class once a semester at Saint Louis University Medical School.

They had an open forum during their genetic class for the medical students to be able to ask questions about living with Turner Syndrome (TS) and how I was diagnosed. Not only did the students find it to be extremely helpful, but also I have the benefit of knowing I have helped in some small way to educate upcoming doctors who will be diagnosing future children with TS. I always stressed the point to them that they may pass a person with Turner Syndrome on the street and not even know it because of misinformation and old stereotypes.

Another ulterior motive of mine for educating doctors is the story I have heard all too many times from women who have just found out from an amniocentesis or ultrasound that their child will be born with TS. This, in itself, is an extremely difficult time for a couple because of the unknown. But then to add even more to a traumatic situation, imagine if the doctor you have had for many years and trusted explicitly told you that you might want to consider terminating the pregnancy because your child was diagnosed with TS. I still wonder about such an option when 98 percent of TS fetuses miscarry on their own during the first trimester. If a mother can get through that first trimester, I believe her baby is a fighter and survivor. Not to say the baby won't have challenges in life, but which one of us doesn't have our own issues, right?

As past president of our local Saint Louis Turner Syndrome Chapter from almost the beginning of its existence, I have talked to many women in this very situation, and words cannot begin to express my anguish. Many times the doctor himself doesn't even know about Turner Syndrome, except what he has read years ago in an outdated medical dictionary or journal that depicts it as something horrible showing grotesque pictures. My heart goes out to these mothers who love their daughters before they're even born and are now torn apart by their doctor's recommendation. I listen with a sympathetic ear when these mothers call me and say they don't know what to do. My response to them is to please come to one of our support group meetings and meet other TS children first. Only then will they realize what a tragedy it would be to miss out on sharing the joy of having and raising such a very special daughter. I have been known to tell some parents that if their child is going to have any syndrome at all, Turner's is the best one to have! Once again, only education is going to help society with the misconceptions about TS. So hopefully by talking to future parents of a TS child, we have put their minds at ease and reassured them that our local support group and our national organization are there every step of the way to support them.

CHAPTER 2

What We Know about Turner Syndrome

Since my diagnosis in 1971, there have been overwhelming medical advances for girls or women with TS. They can now lead completely normal and productive lives. Today TS can be diagnosed through an amniocentesis in the beginning stages of a pregnancy, which gives parents an early advantage to prepare and educate themselves. And within the past twenty-plus years, the availability of the egg donation or in vitro fertilization programs around the United States has given hope to the possibility of pregnancy for TS women. Let's explore what we currently do know about this silent syndrome.

There are approximately sixty thousand to eighty thousand girls or women with Turner Syndrome in the United States and the same amount in Europe and Canada. Considering that 98 percent of TS fetuses spontaneously miscarry during the first trimester of pregnancy, those sixty thousand plus are the 2 percent that survived to term! Can you imagine what kind of numbers we would be talking about if those 98 percent survived? It has always been fascinating to me how Mother Nature works. Thousands of women have miscarriages every year and don't know why. I believe the medical community needs to explore this more closely. It is difficult for me to understand why a doctor would recommend terminating a TS pregnancy. If a baby miscarries on its own during the first trimester, then maybe this is nature's way of taking care of its own (for the severe cases). What mother would not want to give their child a fighting chance to live? If a mother carries past the first trimester, that means that the baby is a fighter and will continue to be one even after she enters this world!

A. Heart/Kidney Issues.

A very common question is "What is Turner Syndrome?" when you first mention to someone you have it. In laymen's terms (because I know from personal experience that my doctor liked to use words fit for dictionary use only), it is a chromosome disorder affecting the forty-fifth X chromosome. This can affect any major organ in the body. Some TS patients have different cases ranging from heart defects—coarctation of the aorta is very common—or kidney problems (horseshoe-shaped kidneys) to very mild cases, such as in my case. You will quickly find out that the severity will vary as much as any one individual does. You cannot stereotype the whole syndrome and say that all TS girls will have all these issues. That is why it is so important to work very closely with your doctor and feel confident with him or her.

Those who have heart problems will most likely be born with a widening of the neck (commonly called webbing). Today cosmetic surgery is an option for those who choose if it is an issue for your daughter. It is also very common for TS babies to be born with edema (swelling of the hands, feet, and/or genital area). This puffiness eventually goes down with time. There are a lot of similar characteristics in girls with TS, but to say TS girls will share all of them is incorrect.

B. Different Karyotypes.

A karyotype test can be done to identify exactly what kind of chromosomal makeup your daughter has. This is normally done by a doctor when an infant is suspected of having TS at birth. Because of the partial or total missing of the X chromosome, most TS girls will also have ovarian failure (otherwise known as gonadal digenesis). There have been reports of a few Turner's women who do not have the typical characteristics of TS (short stature or thick neck), and they have ovulated on their own. There has been a very small percentage of TS women who have ovulated on their own and achieved pregnancy because of the chromosomal makeup they have (meaning she may have enough of the X chromosome for the ovaries to produce eggs). They are in the minority, once again proving that you cannot stereotype the whole syndrome.

C. Taking Growth Hormones.

Another facet of TS I would like to discuss is the human growth hormones that are affected which results in short stature. The pituitary gland in a TS child does not secrete enough growth hormones to sustain a normal growth pattern, so gradually she will start to fall off the normal growth chart for children. This happened to me when I was in approximately the first grade, which is very common. At first, my doctor did not give much thought to my short stature because both my parents were not that big in size. (My father was five feet and ten inches, and my mother was five feet and four inches.) You will see after meeting other TS girls or women that short stature is a common trait, but once again, it can vary as widely and as differently as each individual. (Example, you can have a tall TS person compared to other TS girls if she has two genetically tall parents, but she would be considered very small within her own biological family.)

There are tests to find out if your daughter is growth-hormone deficient or not, which causes the short stature. If she is, there have been wonderful results with growth hormones that have helped TS girls achieve adult heights virtually unheard of less than twenty years ago. They can even predict your child's adult height with amazing accuracy before starting on growth hormones. Growth hormones were not available when I was diagnosed in 1971, but fortunately today, TS girls have so much more available to them to help with short stature.

There are many ongoing studies today showing the emotional and psychological effects of short stature on children. The growth hormones help keep TS children growing, for the most part, at an even pace with their peers (which, as we all know, is so very important when we are going through that stage of acceptance from our peers). As a parent, it is a very big decision whether or not your daughter should take growth hormones. I highly recommend keeping up-to-date with the current status of growth hormone studies by attending the annual Turner Syndrome Society of the United States Conference, which includes guest speakers from all over the world and the United States who are conducting these studies. Your pediatric endocrinologist can also be a great source of information for you. These conferences help educate parents so they can make a well-informed decision on whether growth hormones are the right choice for their daughter or not.

I was diagnosed unfortunately before growth hormones were available. But I firmly believe I would have chosen to take the growth hormones in order to stay within the normal growth pattern with my peers. When I was in middle school, my doctor was trying to postpone putting me on estrogen replacement therapy to start puberty (which is due to the missing X chromosome) because he was concerned taking them may jeopardize reaching my maximum adult height potential. The way it was explained to me was that once you reach puberty, your bone plates start to gradually close, and your height potential could be compromised. But today they have found that they can introduce small doses of estrogen without limiting your child's fullest height potential. In fact, as of December 1996, the FDA approved growth hormones for TS patients. Our national organization worked diligently for more than ten years toward this goal; there is now help with insurance coverage for families taking growth hormones.

D. Dealing with Biases toward Short Stature.

I believe, in today's society, there is an unconscious bias toward adults with short stature. I have come across this numerous times in my business career. I have experienced many job interviews and wondered afterward how much my short stature played a role in the final candidate decision. One interviewer in particular was blatant enough to even suggest that the administrative position in the IVF (in vitro fertilization) program I was interviewing for might be emotionally too much for me to handle. Who better to have the empathy, compassion, and understanding of what these women were going through but someone who has already been through the program? I found this to be extremely patronizing because I would not have interviewed for that position if I wasn't qualified or didn't think I could handle it.

Hopefully this kind of discrimination can be addressed in future annual Turner Syndrome conferences so that positive changes can be made in this area. Our children cannot be raised with the philosophy that "you can't do that" because you're too small. I believe a child needs to go through the experience; otherwise, they will never know if they could have achieved or not. And if afterward they don't succeed, then they feel a lot better about the outcome because they know they did everything possible and tried their best. That's all anyone can ask of one another. It really does help with their self-esteem when they know they have tried their best, and they will become stronger because of it.

One way I have tried to deal with my short stature is with a sense of humor. When the short jokes start, I try to make light of them so as not to put the other person on the defensive, but I do let them know when they have gone too far. One great example of this would be in my workplace environment again. There was a gentleman I worked with for many years. He was a very tall and large person who some may have considered to be loud and obnoxious. (He was six feet and two hundred thirty-plus pounds compared to my four feet and eleven inches and one hundred five pounds!) After getting to know him, I learned his bark was definitely worse than his bite. He was abrasive at times, but deep down, he was a pussycat. One day, as usual, he called me by his favorite nickname. "Hey, Shrimp." You'll find that, for some odd reason, people do not find it disrespectful to have nicknames for small-statured adults. After a while, I felt this was not appropriate in a business professional setting. So one day, in a matter-of-fact tone, I answered him back by saying, "Yeah, what do you want, fatso?" Well, needless to say, there was total silence. I figured if he had the nerve to call me shrimp, then I would see how he liked the tables turned. He thought about it a minute and then proceeded with whatever it was he was saying and never called me shrimp again. He got the hint without ever saying another word. Many years later, I find it interesting that I felt it was even necessary to resort to such a tactic.

E. Estrogen Replacement Therapy.

Psychologically and emotionally for girls, when they are a young teenager and all your peers are developing—and you so desperately want to be like your peers—it is not much consolation to be told you'll have to wait to start estrogen replacement therapy like I was. I can look back today and thank my doctor from the bottom of my heart for the modest adult height of four feet and eleven inches that I was able to achieve because of his careful watch and administration of small doses of a steroid. Both my doctor and poor parents went through turmoil with me during that time though. It is not easy raising a teenager, and then to have to add this emotional hurdle to the process can be quite challenging, as they can attest.

In my later teenage years, I saw my endocrinologist once a year. He was affiliated with a major medical teaching university and had interns who would examine me first before he came in to see me. This added to my anxiety because I was getting older, but these interns were only becoming closer and closer to my age each year! Now you know why I dedicated this book to my family! My parents put up with a lot from me during that critical time in my life, especially going through such emotional issues.

I have talked to several adult TS women who decided a long time ago not to take their estrogen after they found out they could not have children. They figure why bother taking estrogen to have a period every month if they didn't ovulate and couldn't get pregnant. But this is not a healthy decision recommended by doctors. Female hormones affect a lot more than just that. It affects your hair texture, skin texture, and most importantly, it guards against osteoporosis. Doctors are very interested in seeing how the prolonged use of estrogen affects bone density, etc. I encourage anyone who has stopped taking their estrogen for a long time to consult their doctor again about this and even get a second opinion about their decision if necessary.

F.   Dealing with Educators.

Today TS girls can be a normal teenager without the additional burden of worrying if they are going to look like their peers and fit in. I am sincerely grateful to modern medicine and can't begin to tell you what this means to me as a TS adult woman because teens today can now be spared all that I went through as a teen. I also feel that teachers or educators of TS girls need to be made aware and be more sensitive to these issues, as your child is going through that particular stage in her life. Some parents may be hesitant to discuss this with their child's teachers for personal reasons, but I'd like to share with you a story that happened to me to stress that education is the best policy.

I had a gym teacher I'll never forget who gave me trouble all during middle school because my doctor would give me permission slips to be excused from taking showers in gym class. (I was extremely modest about the whole ordeal.) Of course, my other classmates didn't understand why I was being excused, and the teacher added additional stress to the situation by making it clear that I would lose points in gym class for not taking showers. Today TS children do not need to be pointed out as different from their peers. My parents never discussed my TS diagnosis with my teachers that I know of, but I have always wondered if the situation would have been handled differently if my teacher had known all the facts.

G. Rising a Healthy Turner's Child.

I have met several parents of TS girls who have been extremely overprotective while raising their daughter. I guess that was one advantage I had of not being diagnosed until the age of eleven. I was not raised any differently than my siblings. Sometimes it can be a disadvantage for parents if they know the diagnosis from the beginning. It's a normal reaction to want to protect your daughter from this "mean and cruel world" sometimes. Parents should take an active role in the raising of their daughter, but when it becomes inhibitive to the point where a child is not given the opportunity to do or try something because they're viewed as "being too small to do that," then it becomes negative instead of positive. There are some positive points to being small, believe it or not. We as parents should be trying to encourage our children to be productive, secure, and independent individuals. There is no reason your child cannot do or achieve anything they put their minds to (big or small). We have everything from lawyers, CPAs, a retired judge, and RNs in our TSSUS organization. It's all in how you are raised. It can become a self-fulfilling prophecy if you constantly tell your child you can't do that because then they will begin to believe it. They won't feel confident to take risks in life, and you'll miss the ultimate opportunity of watching your child succeed. So, parents, think twice before you give your daughter an answer when she asks you permission to do or try something new. I have this story to share with you.

I had a doctor who was world renowned in endocrinology, and I highly respected his medical opinion, but his bedside manner was the pits! I remember this doctor asking me in my senior year of high school what my plans were after graduation. When I informed him I was going to college to major in nursing, he looked at my parents and said, "Did you know about this? You realize she will have extreme difficulty, and she probably won't make it through nursing school." Well, that made me even more determined. I did graduate after five years with a bachelor of science degree but ended up changing my major to business administration with a minor in French instead because of the long waiting list to get into the nursing program. (By the way, I also have six hours toward my MBA—and hope someday to complete it—but I will always remember his comment.)

Yes, some TS children may require extra assistance getting through classes because of certain learning challenges, but that is still no reason not to try. It can be very easy to use the excuse of having Turner Syndrome for not achieving certain goals in life. But if you do that, you'll never know if you could have succeeded or not if given the chance. So please, parents, be very careful not to fall into that trap. Be as supportive as you can during those times of failures and share in her rejoicing when she succeeds.

H. Dealing with Infertility.

Another extremely difficult time in my life was when my doctor told my parents that I would never be able to have children. My husband and I both come from a large family, and this was a very hard thing for me to accept. Today, with medical advances, the IVF (in vitro fertilization) program is available to TS women. They have had wonderful results, and growing numbers of TS women are achieving pregnancy to date. The doctors in the IVF program that I dealt with all agree that TS women are their favorite patients! It is much easier for them to manipulate a TS woman's cycle in the IVF Program. They can take a TS woman off hormones and then start from the beginning of the next cycle preparing the uterus for implantation with a special protocol of estrogen patches or pills and progesterone shots. As each year passes, they are perfecting the procedure so that the parents of TS babies born today will not have to tell their daughters they won't be able to have a family. It will be more difficult but not impossible. Please make sure to consult your physician, as each individual woman's health situation needs to be considered. There are some TS women with heart conditions that may not be recommended for the IVF program.

After being married five years, my husband and I started the IVF program in 1988 when it first became available in our area. I feel extremely fortunate to have had the opportunity to go through the program because this was not even an option fifteen plus years prior to that. It is so important to at least have this opportunity available, especially for TS women. IVF is not for everyone, but personally, I had to go through it myself so that I knew I did everything possible to start our family. This is just another example of what I was speaking about when I mentioned that parents need to let their children go through difficult experiences in life. I'm sure it was not easy for my family to watch and hear me telling them stories about what the program entailed. It did not work for us, but can you imagine if it had? What a family celebration we would have had!

As I was writing this book, our family did not know this—but they eventually found out—that we were in the IVF program again in 1995. We never thought we would ever be able to go through the in vitro program again because of the financial burden the first time. Both our families were extremely generous and offered to help us financially the first time we went through the program because our insurance did not cover in vitro. (This was in addition to the loans we had to take out for our two adoptions.) That is why we chose not to say anything to our families when the opportunity arose for us to go through it a second time. We didn't think it was fair since they had given us so much already (financially, emotionally, and spiritually). Plus, they probably would have thought we were crazy to consider going through it again after all the physical and emotional trauma we went through the first time. Our family forgave us for not saying anything to them until after we completed the program. We just wanted to spare them all this again. I guess you never know until you go through it yourself what exactly you will do in each situation.

Our second attempt was made possible through our contacts and networking. We were told about a couple who had been through the in vitro program and had extra embryos that they wanted to donate to a couple who couldn't have children. They were blessed to have achieved pregnancy twice and were not going to use the rest of their frozen embryos. Since I worked at the same hospital where this couple's embryos were frozen, it was easy to check on the status to see if it would be possible or not for us to go through the program again.

After much research, we decided we could financially afford to do it because of the generosity of this beautiful couple. I went through many tests and procedures again to make sure everything was optimal before having the procedure done. The tests came back that I had a small fibroid on the uterus about half inch in size. The doctors were not that concerned about it at first. But after going through one trial cycle of hormones that the program requires, the fibroids grew to be three times the size of the uterus. It was putting pressure on my kidneys, which could cause kidney damage and was causing me a lot of back pain. The doctors recommended surgery to remove the fibroid before going through the IVF procedure again.

We were extremely fortunate because the fibroid was removed with no damage to the uterus. That was an extremely emotional time for us because if the doctor should start to remove the fibroid and found it deeply embedded in the uterus, major bleeding could result. A hysterectomy would then have to be performed to stop the hemorrhaging. This, of course, would put us out of the IVF program completely. But our prayers were answered, and the doctors were very pleased the way everything went so smoothly during the surgery.

So six months later after recuperation from that surgery and juggling of the IVF program schedule, we finally arrived at a date to go through another transfer of embryos. I went back on the protocol of estrogen, progesterone, and prenatal vitamins. We can look back today with a sense of humor about taking the hormones. My husband used to say I was Dr. Jekyll and Mr. Hyde when I started on the hormone protocol. There was a noticeable difference in my personality. It was like I could turn mean in seconds and want to pull your hair out for no reason.

I remember quite vividly how much my husband hated giving me the progesterone shots. The nurse taught him how to administer it, but you might have thought he was receiving the shot, not giving it! I was often in an ornery mood on the hormones, so he would remind me who was giving me my shot. Paybacks really do hurt! Just kidding!

I'd like to share my favorite story that keeps both of us laughing, even after all these years. The doctors prescribed Estraderm patches to wear when I started the IVF program the first time. As the weeks progressed, you increased the number of patches you wore on the trunk of your body to mimic a normal cycle. I preferred taking the pills than wearing the patches that were absorbed directly into the bloodstream. The doctors swore they wouldn't come off with normal use, but it was summertime, and they would slide all around with the littlest perspiration. Of course, when that happens, it affects your hormone level, and you experience firsthand what "bouncing off the wall" means.

One morning, I woke up and was missing one of my four patches. I asked my husband Chris to get out of bed and help me find it. We both looked and looked, and then I found it as he turned around to walk across the room. It was stuck to the hairs on the back of his leg! He ran around the room in circles, screaming, "Get this thing off me!" I, jokingly in a high-pitched voice, said, "Hi, Chrissy!"

The day finally arrived to have the embryo transfer again. We waited patiently as we went to work that day while they thawed the frozen embryos. Then the phone call came. All four embryos had survived the thaw! It was highly unusual that all the embryos would survive, so the doctors were very pleased. They cannot tell you how many or which ones may survive a thaw. There is always the possibility that none would survive. So we left work early that day and went to the outpatient surgery area to have the transfer done. They rolled in the incubator with the four embryos before the transfer was done to let us see them through a microscope. It was truly amazing to see these living embryos and realize you may be looking at your own child before he or she is even born! Nobody can convince me that God doesn't exist! You would be prolife too if you experienced what we did.

Sometimes it feels like we're on a roller-coaster ride, and it doesn't stop. I felt compelled to write about this experience so that maybe in some small way, it could give hope and encouragement to other TS women. I have been able to share and speak to other TS women at our annual national TS conferences who have told me their heartwarming IVF stories. This opportunity has allowed us to be a source of strength for each other since we all went through similar experiences. It is dramatic to hear each of these women's stories. You really realize that you're not alone when you're able to share like that. We were able to discuss every aspect of the different IVF programs together and have compassion beyond understanding for each other. I was fortunate enough to even be invited to speak at the annual Canadian Turner Syndrome Conference in 1989 about my first IVF attempt.

In the beginning years when IVF was first introduced, no insurance companies would pay for this procedure. At that time, they considered it experimental (even though they were having good results in Europe). My employer medical insurance informed me that they did not pay for anything associated with the IVF program. But during my research, I found out that they did pay for artificial insemination. Immediately it made me wonder what kind of message this was sending. My own personal interpretation was that if my husband had the infertility problem, they would pay for us to use artificial insemination in order for us to start our family. But since I had the infertility issue and we needed an egg donor, they weren't going to pay for it since it was so expensive.

This upset us so much that we decided to go through the appeal process with my insurance company. I proceeded to the very highest level of the appeal process, which they called arbitration. It was recommended that my husband and I be accompanied by our lawyer going into the arbitration meeting. Of course, being young and naïve, we decided we could not continue any further.

We had already spent our life savings on the IVF attempts, and hiring a lawyer would be very expensive to continue the appeal process. It would have been a great step forward for not only TS women but also all women needing IVF in the state I lived in. Looking back now and being much wiser and stronger, I wish we had completed the appeal to the end. I know deep down that we could have set precedence, won this case, and changed our state laws.

IVF has become a topic that even TS teenagers want to hear about. They can learn so much from our experiences; and someday, hopefully, they will not have to deal with the obstacles that we, as beginning pioneers, had to endure. I'm speaking about fighting insurance companies, not only for other areas of TS such as growth hormones but also for the IVF program.

I really enjoy talking to the teens during our teen program at the annual national TS conferences because they are filled with so many wonderful questions, especially about dating. One commonly asked question is, "How do you know when the right time is to tell your boyfriend that you have TS?" I respond that everyone is different. It's not something you tell every man you date, but you'll know when the right time is for you. Then I share my story as an example of the night I told my boyfriend (now husband) that I had TS.

My husband and I started dating during my junior year in college. We dated two years and were engaged a year before we got married. The first year we dated, I had to go back to Saint Louis for my annual checkup and get a refill on my estrogen prescription. He couldn't understand why I just couldn't see a doctor there in the small college town where we were instead of having to make a trip back to Saint Louis. After a year of dating, I still hadn't told him that I had TS. I insisted that I had to see my doctor who was a specialist I had been seeing for years. He got very worried, and without my knowledge, he called my mother and asked her all sorts of questions about my doctor and why I had to see this particular doctor, etc. When I arrived home, my mother sat me down and told me that he had called and was very upset because he thought I was terminal with something. I guess you could say my mother knew even before I did that he was serious about me. It was at that point that I realized I had better tell him the truth. Everyone is different, but you'll know when the right time is for you.

My husband majored in social work and wanted to work with juveniles, so I knew how much he loved children. I became very scared all of a sudden when I realized that I took the chance of losing him by telling him I had TS. I assumed he couldn't accept the fact that he would not be able to have his own children if we stayed together. Boy, did he blow my theory of most men! When I eventually got the courage to tell him, I was stunned by his response. He told me that he knew firsthand there were a lot of children out there that needed good homes from working with so many of them in the juvenile court. We could still have the family we both dreamed of by adopting. I asked him how he felt about not having his own children. I really wanted to know and truly cared about his feelings. He told me that if he had to choose between going through life with me or without me, there was no choice. And if it meant having to adopt to have our family, then that's what we would do. That was the most romantic thing I had ever heard. Now you know why I married him!

I still don't understand why the desire in me was so strong to go through the IVF program, but I knew that I had to do it. I guess this was a way of putting my mind at ease that we did everything possible to have a family, not only for me but for my husband too. After completing the program unsuccessfully for the second time, it made us even more positive that our decision to adopt was the right choice. We now knew we had done everything we could, and God had a child out there that needed us. He just had to lead us to this child, which He eventually did.

I. The Adoption Search.

One blessing in all this is that we would not have our beautiful son today if the IVF had worked the first time in 1989. We would not have been searching for an adoption lead. We adopted our son in 1991 through a private adoption in between both our IVF attempts. This is another extremely difficult option for TS women because you are in the adoption search with the other thousands of couples in the United States dealing with different infertility problems. It took an additional seven years after our son's adoption of actively pursuing adoption leads to find our second child. But because we kept up with our networking, we had many leads during those years. Networking is how we got our son. I cannot begin to stress how important networking is in the adoption search. Let me tell you our first adoption story.

We went through the adoption agency route with all their rules and regulations when we first got married. One rule was you couldn't list with them until you were married for two years. That was our only option to start a family before IVF came along. We eventually got to list after the two years, but they had a five- to seven-year waiting list. Since we knew we wanted to adopt when we first got married, we figured we'd list with an agency immediately. As was standard policy, the agencies told us that their fees were nonrefundable when we listed with them. That was not a problem because we knew we were going to adopt. They tell you that because many couples finally list with an agency after dealing with years of infertility. Soon after that, when the pressure is off and they accept and embrace the idea of adoption, they find out they are pregnant. Then they want their money back. But that was not our case because of having TS.

We even went as far as strategically putting ads in local newspapers in areas that were very prolife but economically challenged and even college towns. We had our phone number changed and unlisted so that we could receive calls from those responding to our newspaper ad. It was quite an ordeal. Overall, the majority of calls we received seemed legitimate. I believe we only received one crank call in all that time. There was one call, though, that I will never forget.

In the beginning when we first were researching how to put an adoption ad in the newspaper, I called around to get price quotes to run an ad for cost comparison and sales volume. A friend of mine called me one evening to see if I had gotten any responses yet from our ad. I informed her that we had only gotten price quotes so far and had not run the ad yet. She then stated that she was looking at our ad in that evening's newspaper! I was shocked! It was required that you read your ad to them over the phone first before they could give you a price quote since it was based on the number of words. Someone had made a big mistake and ran the ad anyway.

Well, needless to say, I was very upset. From all the books I had read, when you run an adoption ad for a private adoption, you are supposed to have an adoption lawyer already lined up and have a certain list of questions next to the phone ready to ask prospective birthmothers when they call. At that time, we were still interviewing lawyers and hadn't made our final decision yet, and we had no list of questions ready. After I calmed down from talking to my friend, I decided to take a nice, warm bubble bath to soothe my nerves. You'll never guess what happened next.

You got it. The phone rang when I was in the bathtub! The operator asked if I would accept a collect call from a particular name I didn't recognize. Then all of a sudden, it occurred to me that this could be someone responding to our ad. So I immediately accepted the charges and started to talk to this person. He was just as nervous as I was responding to our ad. My heart dropped. He then asked me if it mattered what the gender of the baby was. I told him no since my husband and I did not have any children. He then proceeded to tell me a story that would break your heart.

He told me of how his girlfriend and he had a baby together after living together for a while. He said they had a little boy who was now three months old. His girlfriend was recently killed in a car accident, and he didn't feel he could raise the child by himself. He said someone had told him to look in the newspaper for adoption ads, if adoption was what he wanted to do. He had never heard of anyone putting adoption ads in the newspaper before. I informed him that it was a relatively new trend in 1990. During our conversation, I had been hearing weird noises in the background but didn't dare interrupt his story.

He then proceeded to tell me that he was not handling his girlfriend's death that well. He had been drinking one night and was arrested for a DWI (driving while intoxicated). He was calling me from the county jail. That was the weird noises I had been hearing. He said he was going to be making arrangements for his son's adoption as soon as he was able to post bail. I then began to worry that he was going to bring up the subject of money. I knew that the state of Missouri was extremely conservative and only allowed adoptive parents to pay for legal and medical costs. Money was one subject we had to handle very delicately when answering calls from prospective birthparents.

I felt like I should have been on the show *Candid Camera* because I quickly jumped out of the bathtub, bubbles and all, and proceeded to pick out a lawyer's name to give him if he was truly serious. If you remember, we hadn't finished interviewing lawyers yet. So the next morning, I had to call that adoption lawyer, introduce myself, and let him know this gentleman might be calling on our behalf.

Later when we got our phone bill, there on the bill was his call, and he had been telling the truth! He did call our lawyer from the jail but didn't leave a forwarding phone number after he posted bail, so our lawyer had no way of getting back in touch with him. I have a feeling that after his girlfriend's family found out what he was thinking of doing, they probably stepped in. That could have become a very messy ordeal for us. I'm convinced that someone upstairs was looking out for us. Now that was a major roller-coaster ride!

We had been telling all our friends and family that we were looking for an adoption lead from the very beginning when we first got married. If they ever came across a prospective birthmother, they all knew to call us immediately. We had spent a lot of time interviewing and researching different adoption lawyers and finally found one that we felt comfortable with. Whenever we would come across an adoption lead, the lawyer would find out for us if the birthmother was serious about adoption or not. He would handle all the details and only contact us if he thought we had given him a viable lead. Like I mentioned before, we came across many, many leads during our search. You never know which lead might be the one. Our philosophy was that you pursue every lead but never expect anything from it. That way, you don't get disappointed. Otherwise, you would go crazy on what I call the emotional adoption roller-coaster ride.

I have to give you a little background history on our first adoption because it is truly an amazing chain of events that made me a believer in miracles.

I was very close to my great-aunt who was a wonderful religious woman with her own special quirks. She loved wearing her polyester pants and pink puffy slippers, didn't like wearing her dentures, and was a chain-smoking bingo or card player. She had the biggest heart of anyone I knew. She was very protective of me and my husband because she knew how much we wanted to adopt and how long we had been searching. Being the deeply religious woman she was, she told me to pray a novena to Saint Gerard of Majella (the patron saint of mothers) and wear a medal she was going to mail me, and we would get our child. She loved my husband so much because he would take the time to play cards with her all night long when we would visit her. He was used to working the night shift, so it was no big deal for him to do that, but you could tell that she really appreciated the time we spent with her.

Well, of course, I could not break a promise, so I prayed the novena and wore the medal. One month later in February of 1991, we received a call from her. Her granddaughter (my third cousin) knew of a prospective birthmother who seemed interested in adoption. They had met in a home for unwed mothers. My cousin decided to keep her baby, but this birthmother was looking for a simple adoption and didn't want to go through all the rules and regulations of an agency. I gave my great-aunt our lawyer's name and phone number to pass onto my cousin, as was the usual routine on a lead (of course, not expecting anything to materialize). I asked her the name of the home for unwed mothers so I could tell our lawyer where the prospective birthmother would be calling from. When my great-aunt told us the name was Saint Gerard's Home, we knew this was truly a sign from above. We were able to adopt our son four months later through a private adoption when he was only ten days old. This was a true miracle for us and proved that networking does work. I kept a diary during this whole time, and I will share it with him someday when the time is right.

I want our son to know how much he was wanted and how special he was to us. People say how lucky he is to be a part of a family that loves him so much, but actually, we are the lucky ones. He has enriched our lives and brought us so much joy that we know it is not coincidence how he came into our lives. My husband and I firmly believe he is a true gift from God and was picked to be a part of our family long before he was ever conceived. No child is a mistake because God doesn't make mistakes. I look forward to the day when I can meet his birthmother again and give her a hug and thank her from the bottom of our hearts for the ultimate gift of life and love. I hope she realizes what a truly wonderful and totally unselfish thing she did by choosing an adoption plan for her son, whom she loved so much.

It was not easy waiting those four months, wondering if our birthmother was going to change her mind or not. Even though during this whole time she kept telling us she was positive that adoption was what she wanted for her baby, we didn't know what to think. How could she be so sure? That part was very scary. Our lawyer made the arrangements, and we agreed to pay her medical bills, lawyer bills, and the baby's medical expenses, which were allowed in our state.

When we were told that our birthmother's doctor wanted her prenatal fees paid in advance, we needed our lawyer's expertise on the best way to protect us. So many couples lose their life savings paying all their birthmother's bills only to find out at the end the birthmother changed her mind and backed out. Our lawyer came up with a very good solution that protected all parties involved and was also agreeable to the doctor. An escrow account or trust fund would be set up in the amount of the doctor's fees with the understanding that the money would be released to the doctor immediately upon the signing of termination of parental rights by the birthmother. If papers were not signed, she was responsible for her own medical bills.

We also needed our lawyer to assist us with interstate compact approval because we were dealing with two different states. (Our son was born in a different state from where we lived.) We could not take our son out of the state where he was born until we had interstate compact approval from both states; otherwise, it would be considered kidnapping. That's why it is so important to have a lawyer that is not only highly reputable but knows adoption laws extensively. Interstate compact can be confusing, especially to a layperson like you and me. In simple terms, interstate compact reviews the laws of both states involved to make sure there are no conflicting laws.

We got the call at two o'clock in the morning on June 7, 1991, that our birthmother was in labor and was being brought to the hospital. Try to go back to sleep after receiving a call like that! We proceeded to go to work as usual that morning knowing that we were going to be parents at any time. Well, by the time I walked into my office at seven thirty that morning, my phone was ringing. My coworkers were wondering why I grabbed the phone so fast. Up to this point, my husband and I did not want to know the baby's gender, even though our birthmother *really* wanted to tell us. All we wanted to know was that both mother and baby were healthy. When I answered the phone, the social worker asked if we now wanted to know what we had. I told her yes, of course. She gave us all the wonderful details about our little baby boy and told us everyone was doing great. That is a phone call I'll never forget.

I immediately called my husband, and tears streamed down as I told him he was a proud father of a baby boy. I wish we could have been together at that moment to hold each other, but the silence on the phone said everything. We had waited seven years for this moment, and it was finally here.

Since we were obviously anxious to get on the next plane to see our son, our lawyer told us we could take custody of him, if we were willing to do what's called an at risk placement. This meant that since the birthmother had not yet signed termination of parental rights, we ran the risk of her taking him back after he had been placed with us. We decided we would wait to take custody. We had to wait ten long days for the judge to return from his vacation in order to set a court date. Meanwhile, our son was placed in foster care. But we were on the next plane as soon as we got the call that she had signed papers. Our birthmother went over the details of the termination of parental rights with the judge in his chambers to make sure she understood everything and answered any of her questions. I'm sure people were wondering why we were carrying an empty car seat on the plane. But it wasn't empty when we came home with our beautiful son.

Immediately after this, we started networking again for our second adoption. Our son needed a brother or sister! We were extremely excited to find out that the government was offering up to a $5,000 tax credit for adoptions effective January 1, 1997. This came in handy when we finally went through our second adoption. Since we were unsuccessful in achieving a second private adoption for six years preceding our son's adoption, we decided to go internationally to China. After much soul searching and investigation in early 1996, we spent two months putting a dossier together for that country. The People's Republic of China at that time was one of the top countries for U.S. couples to achieve an adoption quickly. The wait was only six months long compared to a five- to seven-year waiting list for United States adoption agencies.

At that time, the rapidly growing population problem in China had created such a situation that the government mandated that urban couples could only have one child and rural couples a maximum of two children. If you had more than one child, you could lose your job, housing, insurance, etc. If your first child happened to be a girl, it was common for couples to leave their baby at an orphanage so they could try again for a boy instead of losing everything they owned. Our hearts went out to that country and the dire need they had to place all these children in orphanages. We thought this was where God wanted us to go but later found out He had other plans for us.

We were one of the next couples to get an assignment for our child from China when there was a dramatic policy change in late 1996. China was going to merge their two adoption departments into one. During all this restructuring, they cut their staff in half. This created a major delay in processing of all paperwork. There had always been the policy in China that couples who already had a child must take a special needs child for their second child. This was never strictly enforced though since there were so many healthy children in the orphanages.

Because of a TV story about Chinese orphanages that aired in November 1996, there was a flood of adoption applications from the United States and other countries coming into that office. It was at that time they began to strictly enforce their policies. They would now only place babies with couples who were under the age of thirty-five and childless. We were over thirty-five and had our five-year-old son at that time. The director of our agency assured us that after the new office had been established, things would go back to the way they were. He said he never saw any policy last too long in China, and it would change again. We just had to be patient and wait.

Our hearts were broken, not to mention our pocketbooks. We had already paid out a lot of money to get to this point, and there were no refunds of course. Fortunately, our agency was willing to work with us. We wanted to be fair to all parties involved, and since the agency had already done work on our behalf, we settled on an equitable amount for their fees, and they refunded the difference to us. But now what do we do? Well, here again, where there's a will, there's a way.

As I mentioned before, networking for adoption is very important. Right after our first adoption was completed, we put out the word to many different adoption agencies all over the United States that if they ever came across a Turner Syndrome child for adoption to please let us know. It just so happened that I received a call in October 1996 about a little girl with Turner Syndrome in a Bulgarian orphanage. We already had money down and were ready for our assignment to China at that time, so we could not afford to do both adoptions. I contacted a very close friend of mine in our local Saint Louis Chapter of the Turner Syndrome Society who said she and her husband would be thrilled to adopt this child. I was so excited for my friend since this would be their first child and also that we would still be able to be a part of this little girl's life, even if we wouldn't be adopting her. In her picture we were given in October 1996, she had jet-black hair, the biggest brown eyes, and longest lashes we'd ever seen. She was born in January of 1995, so she was almost two years old.

I proceeded to help my friend start all the necessary paperwork to get the process going. A group of coworkers of my friend called one of the local Saint Louis TV stations, and they came and did a human-interest story on her. The story was about a Turner Syndrome woman and her husband adopting a Turner Syndrome child. Since I was president for our local chapter, I set up a trust fund at our local bank for people to be able to donate to help defray costs in getting the little girl here to the United States. This also was a great opportunity to educate the public about Turner Syndrome.

The following month, in November 1996, was when we received word that China had closed their doors on us. Not knowing, simultaneously my friend and her husband had made the heartbreaking decision that they could not continue with this adoption for financial reasons. When they called to tell us, we were in shock because we had just received word two days earlier about China, and we hadn't had a chance to tell them yet. My friend's response was overwhelming after we learned of each other's predicament. She said to me in a solemn voice, "If we cannot have her, we do not want anyone else to have her except you. Please tell us you're going to adopt this little girl." By that time, we were both crying on the phone.

Where God closes a door, He opens a window. It's not coincidence the way that both our adoptions happened. No one can convince me that these adoptions were pure luck. Our children were part of God's ultimate plan to be a part of our family from the very beginning. I just wish we didn't have to wait so long for both of them.

We immediately started a whole new dossier for the country of Bulgaria. Just when you think nothing else could happen, it does. Anyone dealing with an international adoption can tell you their roller-coaster story, and here is ours.

Part of the Bulgarian dossier requires that both parents have a complete physical and drug test. That is not considered part of an annual physical according to my insurance company, so I would have to pay for it out of pocket. Then I found out it cost $500 per person ($1,000) for a blood drug test. Needless to say, this was extremely upsetting and an added expense we weren't anticipating. It got to the point that I thought about calling my primary care physician and telling him I thought I had a drug problem just so we could get the referral for the test. But through perseverance and explaining the situation, I was finally able to have my primary care physician give me the needed referral for the test to be covered. This is just another example of the many insurance obstacles that TS families can expect to endure.

I'm sure that each one of the families in our support group can tell you an insurance horror story dealing with everything from growth hormones not being covered at that time (which cost approximately $3,300 per month) to in vitro fertilization (IVF) also not covered back then. Since that time, there have been changes to insurance coverage for IVF, and they will now cover certain procedures in the program (but not the whole procedure). At that time, there was legislation mandating that insurance companies cover IVF for everyone (not just for TS women) in the states of Illinois, Massachusetts, and other states.

The roller-coaster ride continued for us because after completing our dossier in just five weeks, we found out the agency escort service to bring our daughter to the U.S. was being discontinued by the Bulgarian Government in January 1997. Once again, this was totally unexpected, as we were planning to have our daughter escorted to New York. Now we were told we would have to go there to pick her up. We had to play the waiting game as they decided to make an exception or not in our case since they had labeled our daughter "special needs" because of having TS.

In addition to that, we also found out that the Bulgarian Ministry of Justice and Health received our dossier, but our home study was for China. Our agency had put an addendum to our home study, stating we were now going to Bulgaria, but they wanted the original home study to say Bulgaria. They were requesting a whole new home study to be done with the country of Bulgaria on it.

We couldn't believe it. No specific reason was given as to why they would not accept our agency's addendum. At that time, the average cost of a home study was $1,200. We could not afford to have another home study done, especially when there was nothing wrong with the one we had. We could not understand why our dossier was sent to Bulgaria if the agency knew they wouldn't accept addendums. Once again, we worked diligently through this obstacle. Since none of our information had changed, the agency agreed to redo our home study by pulling up our file in their computer and updating the country to read China instead of Bulgaria at no cost. We still needed to pay though for the criminal background checks, all the notary, certification fees, and federal express charges associated with having it processed again. We really appreciated all the parties involved who helped us complete our whole dossier and redo our home study as fast as possible.

The following month, in April 1997, we received a second videotape of our daughter from the Bulgarian orphanage. The first one came in early December 1996. It was taped only three weeks after her heart surgery to repair her coarctation. She looked healthy and seemed to be a lot more energetic than before her surgery. Her stamina and color looked great. But the videotape taken in April 1997 showed a completely different little girl. She looked weak and skinny, and her eyes were sunken. She was still not walking even at the age of two. She was developmentally delayed because of the surgery, and no one was giving her the attention she so desperately needed. She curled up into the fetal position when the caretaker at the orphanage picked her up in the video. Both my husband and I could not bear to watch the video again and immediately called the agency to express our concern. We wondered what kind of care, if any, she was getting (other than being fed and changed). They, of course, wanted us to know that they shared in our concern but that the government was causing our delay, not the agency. They said they would try to get a special nurse or therapist to work with her individually since they knew she was going to be coming to the United States to be adopted. In our opinion, that's all well and fine, but shouldn't they have been doing that from the very beginning?

We informed the agency that we would appreciate if they would use any connections or influence they had to get our paperwork pushed through as fast as possible. We felt like the government was jeopardizing her well-being the longer they delayed us. We were extremely upset because we had all sorts of support set up for her in Saint Louis to help with her developmental delays, and all they did was put up roadblocks. Unfortunately, we were at their mercy and had to wait for our home study to be redone. It normally took four to six weeks for a criminal background check to clear (part of the home study) from the state capital, so that put her developmentally behind even further.

We were desperately trying to think outside the box and come up with unique ideas to get our daughter here sooner. Then my husband remembered that his mother's side of the family was Russian Orthodox, and he had a relative who was an Orthodox priest who may have connections back to the church in Eastern Europe. We were hesitant to ask if he could help us in any way because we weren't sure what the relationship was between the church and government in Bulgaria. We decided to ask our agency first to see if this could be an option to help us push our paperwork through faster.

After speaking to them, we found out that until approximately 1995, Bulgaria was Communist. They are now calling themselves Socialist, but the same party members were still in power, and things were being run exactly the same as before. The only change was in name only. Religion was illegal during Communism, so the government did not recognize any church. It would actually do more harm than good for us to pursue having the church intercede on our behalf.

Shortly after that, we learned that Bulgaria had a new prime minister who was requesting additional information for our dossier. The information he was requesting was already in our home study, but he wanted it separate from the home study. This entailed going back and getting what was originally requested, having it notarized, authenticated, and certified from our Consulate in Washington DC and then Federal Expressed back to Bulgaria. During the winter months of

December and January, the offices close in Bulgaria for the holiday. We continued to wait from December 1997 through January 1998 for all the paperwork to be processed in order to get a court date.

Once that was completed, the court date took place. Apparently, the courts were questioning why there was no effort made to have a Bulgarian family adopt our daughter. After much deliberation, it was determined that every effort was made, and they had termination of parental rights from both birthparents. Because the birthmother's name had changed since papers were originally signed three years prior, they had to go back and locate her to verify that the person's name on the termination papers was the same person—another delay.

Words cannot begin to describe the frustration we felt during this time. You wonder how these three years of living in a Bulgarian orphanage will affect her future in all aspects, especially physically and emotionally. We prayed together as a family every night before we went to bed that God would protect her and hold her tight until the day we could get her here. I look back and remember the first picture we got of her with her two little fingers crossed on both hands. It was like she was saying to us, "Please don't give up. I'm keeping my fingers crossed you'll adopt me." That one little picture kept us going throughout the two-and-a-half-year ordeal.

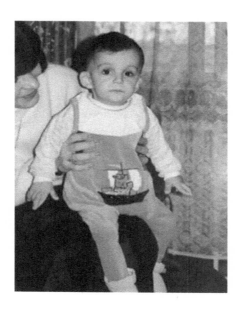

As if it wasn't enough, we were informed by our agency in Minnesota that they would be discontinuing their business relationship with our liaison in Bulgaria after they completed the adoptions they already had on file. We were not given any details other than the liaison wanted the country fees of $6,000 paid up front before our daughter's arrival instead of afterward as originally planned. We informed them that we were not going to pay until services were rendered. The agency agreed that they would prepay the country fees on our behalf, and we could reimburse them upon arrival of our daughter since they were the ones that chose not to continue doing business with this liaison. We agreed to that.

After all that, we received word that they would not allow our daughter to be escorted, and we would have to go to Bulgaria to get her. This would be an additional expense of airfare, hotel, food, etc. We were very disappointed but were determined that this was not going to stop us. Our flight arrangements and hotel accommodations were made for us to coincide with two other couples who were going to Bulgaria from the same agency in New Jersey. We were given a list of dos and don'ts, some local customs, and things for us to bring. We were asked to bring different size of clothes and shoes for our daughter just in case one size didn't fit. The items we brought that didn't fit could be donated to the orphanage. In fact, the need was so great that we were told our daughter could not leave with anything, not even the shirt on her back.

Our social worker coordinated to have the liaison meet us and the other two families when we landed in Bucharest, Romania. All we had were their names but no other information about the other couples who would be travelling with us, so we were anxious to meet them. When they finally gave us our traveling date, we couldn't believe it. We would be gone on our son's seventh birthday! What a birthday present we would be bringing back for him though!

The night before we were to leave, we tucked our son into bed and said our night prayers as usual. We explained to him that he would be staying with Grandpa and Grandma for the weekend starting the Friday we departed and then his aunt and uncle during the week we were gone. He looked forward to being spoiled by his grandparents and playing with his cousins on the farm. He was getting all sorts of attention. We talked to him about why he couldn't come with us (even though he still didn't understand). He expressed deep concern and asked us what would happen if the plane crashed. We told him not to worry and kept telling him how much we loved him. As the tears came down, we told him his family would always be there for him if anything did happen to Mommy and Daddy but not to think negative. We were coming home with a very special birthday present just for him. Because we weren't going to be there on his actual birthday, I even had a special birthday wish go out to him from his favorite radio station that he liked to listen to!

We left Saint Louis, Missouri, on Friday morning, June 5, 1998, to board our flight to New York JFK Airport. Months before we left, I went to several different stores asking for donations to bring with us to the orphanage. I received everything from clothes, diapers, toiletries, to medicine samples from our pediatrician's office. We ended up with four big boxes. We marked them clearly for U.S. Customs. Unfortunately, when we arrived at the airport though, you could only check in two boxes per person, so we had to leave two boxes behind. We decided to take the medicine and clothes and would figure out how we were going to get the other boxes over there later.

We were nervous when we boarded the flight, and the pictures proved it! The moment had finally arrived, and we were actually leaving after two and a half long years! After we said goodbye to our families, we took a deep breath and boarded the plane. We didn't know what would lay ahead for us or what kind of conditions we would find when we visited the orphanage. They told us the orphanage our daughter was in was an average one for Bulgaria. We would find out later that the other two couples we were traveling with would be adopting from a different orphanage than us.

We landed in New York JFK Airport and had several hours before our next flight departed on Tarom Airlines to Bucharest, Romania. We arrived at our departing concourse early. To pass the time, we decided to browse in some of the nearby shops and relax in the area until they opened the gates. After window-shopping, we returned to the area and saw a couple sitting down with an empty stroller next to them. I whispered to my husband that I bet this was one of the other couples. We were for sure it was them when another couple came up to them and started talking. Since they were from the same agency, they had the opportunity to meet each other prior to this trip. We gradually walked up to them and introduced ourselves. Their agency had told them about us, so they were very excited to finally meet us also. We sat for a little while longer and got to know each other. We talked about everything from the money exchange rate to the food in Bulgaria. There was an instant bond between all three families. We were all running on adrenaline and ready to go get our babies.

We were unfortunately not seated together, so we boarded and took our assigned seats for the twelve-hour flight. Our seat assignments were in the last nonsmoking row before the smoking section. A lot of Europeans smoke, and they were smoking the minute the "No Smoking" sign went off. There were some open seats toward the front, so we moved immediately after takeoff. I got out my diary and started jotting down some of my thoughts during the flight.

The flight went by relatively fast, as we tried to sleep as much as possible. We knew the jet lag would set in once we landed because of Bulgaria being eight hours ahead of our time. As we touched down, everyone began clapping. We deplaned onto what looked like the middle of a large field. There were buses waiting to drive us to the terminal. People were pushing and shoving like a herd of cattle. It was humid, and of course, there was no air-conditioning on the bus. After what seemed an eternity, we finally got off the bus and went into the terminal to get our luggage. As we waited for our luggage, we were observing all the different sights and sounds of this country. Many people smoke there, so people were lighting up their cigarettes in the middle of the hot terminal with no air-conditioning. We also noticed women with bandanas around their heads walking around with small straw brooms sweeping the floor. Their faces showed the years of hard manual labor they had endured. It appeared life was difficult there, and times were tough economically. The airport terminal was old and seemed dark and dingy.

We kept close to the other two couples as we went through Customs since this was their second trip to Bulgaria. Their agency required they go out once to meet the child and then go back later to pick up their child. We thank God we had no problems going through Customs. We got together with the other two couples after completing Customs to meet our liason.

The other two couples introduced us to our liaison outside of Customs, and we loaded up the two cars with all our luggage and boxes.

We had about an hour drive from the Bucharest airport to our hotel. We had to cross over the boarder into Rousse, which included going over the beautiful Danube River. We were nervous when we got to the boarder, but our driver reassured us by saying, "No problem" in a very thick accent several times. We approached the boarder gates, which were guarded heavily by the military with machine guns. We watched from inside the car as our driver spoke to the guards and then proceeded back to the trunk of the car. We assumed they were going to open all our boxes, but instead, we watched as the driver handed them several bags of sunflower seeds. Can you imagine bribing the military with bags of sunflower seeds? We proceeded on through with no problems, and no bags were opened. We later found out that sunflower seeds were considered a delicacy there.

We sat quietly as we watched the sights and sounds of the city. It was amazing to see everything from people riding their bikes in the streets to gypsy caravans being pulled by horses. We also noticed air pollution was a problem there with all the cars using leaded gas. We really had a difficult time going through tunnels with all those cars. Everyone kept their windows opened since there was no air-conditioning, which made the fumes extremely strong. There were outdoor markets on the side of the road where I saw an older woman shopping in a long-sleeved dress and a bandana around her head. It was the middle of summer, and temperatures were in the middle to high eighties.

When we finally arrived at the hotel in Rousse, of course, we were very anxious to visit the orphanage. Our translator or escort, Evelina, informed us that we could visit the orphanage today, but the doctor would not be available to give our daughter the final required physical until tomorrow. We decided because of being so jet-lagged that we would freshen up, rest, and get some supper and go there the first thing in the morning (Sunday, June 7, 1998).

Our hotel room was average, but there was no ventilation in the bathrooms, so mold was an issue. There was an air conditioner in the room, but it didn't seem to put out much cool air at all. We got better results opening the windows.

We got up from our nap around 6:00 p.m. Saturday (their time) and had dinner with the other two couples in the hotel restaurant. We figured if we went to bed at 4:00 p.m. their time, we would be wide awake at 2:00 a.m., so this worked out fine. All six of us had a full course meal, including salads, a main meal of chicken with potatoes and vegetables, and dessert along with wine—all for approximately twenty American dollars. Our translator told us to leave a dollar tip for the waitress. We wanted to leave more, but she insisted that a dollar tip was sufficient. We immediately did what she said since she knew the traditions and protocol of Bulgaria. We learned quickly how important it was to be culturally sensitive when adopting internationally. The last thing we wanted was to come across as arrogant Americans throwing our money around.

We felt bad that the other two couples would not be getting their children until Monday, since their orphanage was a three- to four-hour drive from Rousse.

Sunday morning finally came, and we were both dressed and ready to go in plenty of time. We sat patiently in the main lobby and waited for our translator Evelina to meet us and bring us to the orphanage. We found out our daughter was only about four miles away! We arrived at the orphanage and met several of the caregivers that took care of our daughter. The orphanage was very old and outdated but was clean. It was a very hot day, and of course, there was no air-conditioning there. The orphanage was a brick building, so it seemed even hotter.

The moment finally arrived when they walked her into the office where we were waiting. The caregiver said our daughter had been running down the hall, but when they got to the door, she stopped. She looked inside and saw us. She had this look on her face as she closely watched my husband holding the camcorder. She kept glaring at him and then would quickly look down at the floor. I tried to ease things by holding her and stroking her hands. She eventually made her way over to him and started playing with the hair on his arms, and within an hour, she had warmed up to him. We were informed that she wasn't used to being around men since it was all women that had taken care of her in the orphanage. We brought her a baby doll, but she didn't seem too interested in it. I think it was because she didn't know how to play with toys. After a few minutes of gently talking to her, I was able to pick her up and hold her. You could tell she definitely was not used to being held. She had grown a lot since the last pictures we had seen of her. Her eyes, though, had not changed. They were the biggest, most beautiful brown eyes I had ever seen. She was more beautiful in person than I imagined. The videos we received didn't do her justice.

She was so petite that she was fitting into eighteen- to twenty-four-month-old clothes. She only weighed nineteen pounds and was three and a half years old! We were told in advance to bring clothes to change her into because we would have to leave the clothes she had on there at the orphanage. The only problem was we didn't know her size, so we ended up bringing several different sized outfits and donating the rest to the orphanage.

We knew when we first saw her that we wanted to keep her given name and not change it since she already seemed to be responding to it. Radina was such a beautiful name, and keeping it would allow her to hold onto a piece of her heritage. Plus, we couldn't agree on a girl's name anyway, so it all worked out great!

We learned that she was not eating solid foods yet. The most common dish served at the orphanage was called pourra pourra, which consisted of stale bread, goat cheese, butter, and warm water mushed up together (like a porridge). It took us between three to four months of working slowly and teaching her how to chew before she started eating solids. They also told us she was potty trained, but she was not even interested in the potty. She continued to have diarrhea for almost a year after we got her before her system was used to our food. This was a major challenge and concern considering she also tested positive for giardia (*G. lamblia*, an intestinal parasite). Majority of children in the orphanage had it, but they were not treated. Our pediatrician put her on medicine immediately for two weeks, which cleared it up right away. I'm just worried for the other children who weren't treated. There can be horrible side effects if left untreated.

Her little foot was also swollen when we picked her up. The orphanage wanted us to have it checked out by a doctor there in Bulgaria before we left. We were not surprised considering edema is common in TS children. They took us to the local hospital there in Rousse. When we drove up to the front of the hospital, it was like stepping back a hundred years ago. Since gas was over $6 per gallon at that time, the grass was very high, and the building had the appearance of being abandoned. We walked into this dimly lit hallway and waited to see the doctor with several other families. As we were trying to keep our daughter occupied, we noticed there was a gurney lying on top of a metal frame parked at the end of the hall. It reminded us of something out of the TV show *M*A*S*H*. They used it as a stretcher. We stood there in awe as we continued to look around and saw walls with paint peeling off.

The translator came with us as the doctor looked at her foot. He gave us some cream to put on her foot for the swelling, but we knew it wouldn't help. Only growing with time and massaging would provide relief. The cream wasn't going to hurt her so we went ahead followed the doctor's directions. We had her checked out with orthopedics when we returned to the United States. They fit her shoes with a special insert.

Before then, we had put her in sandals with adjustable Velcro straps. She was so swollen that her foot would completely roll to the one side when she walked.

Evelina told us a couple of months before our departure that they were going to be sending our daughter to Sophia (the capital) for therapy since they knew she was going to be adopted and coming to the United States. She said the caseworkers in Sophia who had been working with her for those two months were very pleased with her progress. The caregivers also noticed a big difference when she returned to the orphanage.

We spent the rest of our first day together at the hotel with the other two couples playing with Radina. We watched carefully as she played with the baby doll we gave her. She would take the baby doll's face and rub her mouth all over it. We believe this must have been some kind of a tactile stimulation phase she was going through at the time. It seemed she loved the feel of the cold plastic on her lips. We had to wash the doll's face several times because of the smell. They didn't have milk for the children—it was very expensive—so yogurt was left at room temperature, and they would drink it the same as milk. You can only imagine what her breath was like if your teeth hadn't been brushed for three years. We also found out after we got her home that both her ears were totally blocked with earwax, which dramatically affected her speech. There wasn't time for brushing teeth or cleaning ears at the orphanage when you're dealing with the number of children they had there (approximately two hundred).

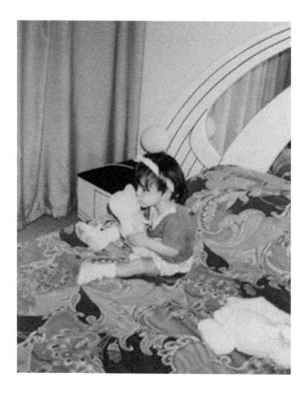

After we picked her up that day and got back to the hotel, we decided to take a walk down the street to an outdoor cafe and ordered lunch. As we were eating, some gypsy children came up to us asking for money. Our translator spoke harshly to them in Bulgarian, and they left. My heart broke as she explained that these children will steal from you, so you have to talk to them sternly because that's all they understood.

After lunch, we took Radina to a park across the street. You could tell she didn't like the swings very much. This could have been related to a spatial differential problem, which is associated with TS. We walked around the main street of Rousse sightseeing and looking at historical statues of the city. We bought Radina two books from there. One was on the history of kings in Bulgaria and the other was a book on the history of Rousse, the town where she was born. We also were able to buy some souvenirs for our families for an extremely reasonable price. (The dollar was very strong then.)

That evening, we had supper in the hotel restaurant. They had a piano player performing, and immediately Radina ran over there. You could tell she loved music, as she twirled herself around in circles as she danced. The other two couples were very anxious for the next day to come, as we were scheduled to travel by van on a three- to four-hour drive to pick up their children at an orphanage in Varna (located by the Black Sea). This would be an all-day trip by the time we arrived back to our hotel that night. We all decided we needed our rest for the big trip and went to bed early. We played with Radina in our hotel room a little more before bedtime. I remember when I sat her on the bed; she looked at me and put her hands on my cheeks as if she was going to kiss me. She seemed to enjoy all the attention she received that day and fell fast asleep in my husband's arms in the chair after experiencing a day she had never had before filled with love.

When everyone was fast asleep that evening, I went down to the front desk and placed an international phone call home to wish our son a happy birthday and tell him about his new sister. I forgot that Bulgaria was eight hours ahead of our time at home! I got an answering machine and left a message for him at Grandpa and Grandma's house. We didn't want him to think we forgot about him. Even if we couldn't be there, we were still thinking of him halfway across the world. So now our son shares his birthday with his sister's "Gotcha Day!"

Early the next morning, we headed to the mountains and countryside of Varna to pick up the other families' children. The roads were full of bright red, yellow, and purple flowers. We saw gypsies in wagons with dogs and goats hooked up to the back traveling on the back roads. We also saw an old woman with a long scarf on her head (it was about 85 degrees out) walking with a big stick and a whole gaggle of geese or ducks in front of her. It was a cultural experience that we truly appreciated and will never forget.

The orphanage in Varna was larger and held older children than the one in Rousse. It placed more children for adoption per year, so it appeared they received a lot more donations than our daughter's orphanage. Rousse only housed children ages newborn to three years old. We used our video camcorder and taped both families as they brought their children into the director's office after giving them baths and changing them into the clothes they had brought for them. The first family got their daughter (twenty-two months old). They changed her name to Maria (a traditional Italian family name). She was full of smiles when they brought her in and played with all the toys. Next was the second family's turn. Their son was an extremely serious little nineteen-month-old boy. He didn't seem to smile much at all. He had a mild cleft palate that had been corrected there in Bulgaria. They also changed his name to an American name, Jordan (different from his birth certificate). We visited and played with the kids in the office while paperwork was being completed. Before you knew it, we were ready to head back to our hotel with all three children!

On the way back to our hotel, we decided to stop and have lunch on the beach. The restaurant was a beautiful big boat on the Black Sea. We walked around barefoot on the beach and let the kids enjoy. After lunch, we took pictures of our families with the beautiful Black Sea in the background.

All the women in our group visited the public restroom before our long trip back home. An employee was stationed out front to collect your two hundred leva (equivalent to ten cents) to use the restroom. She handed us a small piece of rough toilet paper after we paid her! Fortunately, I had a roll of toilet paper from home in my purse, but I made sure to be discreet so as not to offend anyone. This was her livelihood. I walked into the restroom, which consisted of a hole in the ground with two footprints on either side for you to place your feet. Now that was a cultural experience!

The one family had a rough time with their son, as he cried the whole three-plus-hour trip back to the hotel. He would thrash his body backward and cry. They were afraid he was going to bang his head on something, so they took turns watching him carefully. We felt sorry for them, as both these families were first-time parents. We tried to help them out by offering to watch him at times to give them a break when we saw they were stressed out. Our daughter was an angel and slept part of the way. The rest of the time, she would sit on your lap and just watch you in fascination as you spoke to her. She responded more and more to us each day and wanted us to hold her all the time, which was okay with us! Everyone was very tired after that all-day trip.

The next day (June 6, 1998), we met the other families with their children and our translator Evelina for breakfast. There was a cook there that fell in love with the children and tried hard to communicate with us, but she didn't speak English. She fixed them the favorite Bulgarian breakfast of pourra pourra every morning that I mentioned before. We tried experimenting by adding sugar to it one day and bananas to her yogurt. She liked that and really liked orange juice. It was the first time she ever had it. We gradually tried to build her up to eating solids. She would spit out anything clumpy in texture when you gave it to her. You could get her to eat if you mushed up the solids and disguised it in mashed potatoes.

On June 9, 1990, we were scheduled to go to Sophia for the children's passports and visas. This was going to be another long trip, so it would be interesting to see how the kids did. Evelina met us out front of the hotel with a van big enough for all of us. One of the mothers had cassette tapes of children songs, so we played them for a while. Our daughter fell in love with the plastic cover of the cassette and played with it for the longest time, licking it and rubbing her lips all over it just like her doll. Gradually, Jordan was going longer periods without throwing fits or thrashing his head backward.

We arrived in Sophia, which appeared to be a very old city. We noticed the lead gas fumes, which stung our eyes. We had appointments set up for the children's physicals at a nearby clinic and visas. Our translator was a tremendous help with getting all the paperwork ready and setting up all the appointments. The architecture of the buildings were fascinating and reminded me of something from the early 1900s. The pediatrician looked over Radina and said she still needed her MMR shot which we could get back in the United States. The eye doctor said she had pink eye and gave us instructions for that. The ENT doctor said she shouldn't have problems with her ears on the plane ride home. At that time, we didn't know it, but she had a hole in her eardrum which definitely helped with the air pressure. He said we could give her a piece of candy to suck on if we wanted. We thought that was not a good idea considering she wasn't even eating solid foods yet! She'd choke for sure.

There were two different American families at the same clinic going through an adoption at the same time as us. We were told this was the best clinic around. The exam room was furnished with a desk and chair and an old metal exam table with a white cloth over it. It was scary to think Radina may have had her coarctation repaired under these conditions. Next, we went to a photo lab to have pictures taken for their visas. Bulgarian visas required that it show the child's right side with the right ear showing.

We were instructed to come back at 4:30 p.m. that afternoon to pick up our visas. When we looked at Radina's visa, we noticed it had an M for her gender. We immediately told Evelina, our translator and lawyer. Our packet for immigrations had already been sealed, and we were not allowed to open it. She was able to attach an addendum to the packet which we prayed wouldn't cause a problem. We arrived back in Rousse about 11:00 p.m. after a very exciting and long trip that Wednesday (June 10, 1998). The plan was to start out for Bucharest, Romania, on Thursday since our flight left Friday morning.

Evelina had two cars waiting for us for our adventure back to Bucharest. Our flight back to the United States was definitely eventful. You learn very quickly that traveling requires an extreme awareness of cultural differences. We quickly learned about how prevalent discrimination was against the gypsy society. We saw it firsthand, as I mentioned before, with the children asking for money when we were eating outdoors at a cafe, but it really hit us when we went to board our plane back home. The flight attendant greeting us was looking at each of our boarding passes and passports and visas. When it finally came time for our first meal, we were all eventually served, except for one of the families we were travelling with. Their daughter had a gypsy name on her paperwork, and so they were not served the whole flight! We and the other family we were travelling with ended up sharing what food we had with them. Although we could not prove it, you could sense that gypsies were treated differently. We felt compelled to say something to them on the flight, but calmer heads prevailed. We didn't want to make any trouble before getting our children home safely.

When we finally arrived at Saint Louis Lambert Airport, we were surprised. My mother had put out a press release letting the local TV stations know about our arrival and the story of an adult TS woman and her husband adopting a TS child. ABC News showed up and was there to interview us! We had both sides of the family there along with our friend who was originally going to adopt Radina. I was so embarrassed, as I had a green egg in the middle of my forehead from hitting it on the protruding faucet when I leaned over to brush my teeth in our hotel room. And all three of us came down with pink eye from the orphanage the day after getting Radina since we were kissing all over her. You can only imagine what my parents were thinking when we deplaned. My mother took one look at me and said, "I'm never letting you leave the country again!" We wouldn't change one single thing about this remarkable trip of a lifetime.

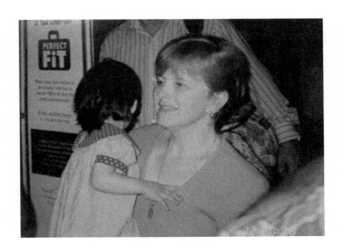

My son has known from the beginning that he was adopted. He didn't fully understand what it meant at first, but he eventually starting asking us about it, and we told him his beautiful adoption story. Since he heard the word *adoption* used a lot in such a positive light, it was not such a traumatic thing to learn he was adopted. The same principle I believe applies to telling your child about having Turner Syndrome. We handled it the same way with our daughter. We just had two subjects to talk to her about instead of one.

Getting Active in a Support Group

Growth hormones, insurance problems, IVF, and adoption are just some of the topics we cover in our local support groups and the TSSUS organization. It really makes things easier for you not only as a parent but also as an individual with TS when you can share with others your experiences of living with TS. I have learned so much from other parents and adult TS women by listening to their concerns and fears. I find it is essential to have a support group available, especially for newly diagnosed families. I have been able to share my ordeals and pain going through the in vitro program with other TS women who were in the same situation as me at our annual TSSUS conferences, and I can't begin to tell you how much this has helped me. We share a bond today that no one else could begin to imagine. I have made many lifetime friends and wouldn't trade them for the world. We have shared together our hopes and dreams of the future for TS babies born today.

I can't count the number of times I have heard the comment "I thought I was the only one with TS. I never knew there was anyone else out there! Where was this support group years ago when I needed it?" I was twenty-four years old before I ever met another individual with TS. Needless to say it was overwhelming for me and my parents. They could have really used a support group when they were raising me during those difficult teenage years.

A support group can also help parents deal with the never-ending insurance problems they will encounter. Our group has come up with some innovative solutions. (Don't forget, numbers count!) Because everyone has different insurance plans, we are learning from each other what works and what doesn't. An example of this would be that after some of the parents started sharing stories about their insurance company nightmares, they learned it was very important to work closely with their child's physician, especially when submitting claims to their insurance company. It may mean the difference between a claim being paid or not depending on how your doctor submits the claim to your insurance company. Many parents have become insurance experts along the way and end up educating their doctors! With healthcare reform possibly changing our current healthcare system as we know it, it is essential we make our needs be known as our child's strongest advocate.

Also, many parents of TS children are not aware until they speak with other parents that there is financial options available out there for them. For example, for those families who want their daughter to start growth hormones but cannot afford it because it is not covered under their insurance plan, help is available. Some pharmaceutical companies obtain federal grants each year and are able to offer assistance to families who would otherwise not be able to purchase growth hormones for their daughter. This is just one of the many areas we touch upon in our local support group. Your national TSSUS organization can be a wealth of information and will direct you where to go if a question arises that we cannot answer on the local level. We encourage sharing of information you may come across during your research with others on the local and national level. This enables us to work through any obstacles that families may come across and not have to keep reinventing the wheel.

The support group is a source of strength for every age group dealing with Turner Syndrome, whether you are a parent of a TS child, teenager, or an adult TS woman. When we have our meetings, we may have a guest speaker on a specific topic geared to a certain age group or just an informal meeting where I may announce any new topics and open the meeting for discussion. We have even had social gatherings to provide the opportunity for the children or adults to get to know each other and learn and have fun at the same time.

CHAPTER 3

What to Expect during the Different Stages of Your Daughter's Growth

Infancy.

Today, with the availability of the amniocentesis, future parents can receive an early diagnosis of many different chromosomal disorders, including TS. One advantage of this kind of information is that it gives parents time during the pregnancy to educate themselves and prepare for the challenges ahead. It may seem like you are running to the doctor a lot at first, but don't be discouraged. After many years of discussion, our local support groups and national organization have gotten together to create TS clinics around the United States. You now have the opportunity for your child to be seen by several specialists on clinic day instead of having to take her out of school for each separate doctor appointment. It is a coordination of services that is efficient and will assist in the overall care of TS patients. It has also enabled us to bring together the top endocrinologists, cardiologists, and other specialists from around the United States who are now interested in forming a national research database for TS patients. Research studies have provided doctors a wealth of knowledge about TS, and the quality of care for TS patients continues to improve annually.

Your daughter will need medical attention at first, depending on her individual situation. As you read and learn more about TS from your pediatrician, through the Internet, and receive information from your local groups and national organization, it will give you a solid foundation for the support you will need. Please do not feel you are all alone in this journey. Don't be afraid to reach out to other TS families in your local support group. Medical advances have given TS children the opportunity to lead a normal and productive life. Sometimes adjustments will have to be made along the way according to your child's needs, but it's a miracle to see your child blossom and be able to achieve their fullest potential. All things become clear, and all the fear and sacrifices you make as a parent melt away when she looks into your eyes with unconditional love.

Preschool.

As your daughter reaches preschool age, ear infections may become an issue. There are several reasons for this. It may become necessary to work closely with an ear, nose, and throat (ENT) doctor to evaluate her situation. Your child's daycare will need to be kept advised of all medications and doctor's instructions. During this time, your child's endocrinologist will be watching her growth closely. Every child is different, but sometime between the ages of three to seven, the endocrinologist will recommend starting growth hormones when she starts to fall off the growth chart. You will notice that parents of TS children in this age bracket will be searching for information on growth hormones and wanting to speak to other families who are currently on growth hormones. Your local support group can help put you in touch with families in your area.

School Age (Grades 1 to 8).

Before your child starts elementary school, you may want to research your school district to find out what kind of rating it has. It is extremely important to have constant communication with her teachers. Depending if your child has a hearing issue or not, special arrangements can be made in the classroom for her. Hearing loss can greatly affect all aspects of learning. Your school district should be able to provide the necessary resources for your daughter. An IEP (individual educational program) through the special school district can assist in setting up any and all additional programs that she may need.

Another critical emotional stage will be when your daughter reaches the lovely middle school age. She will begin to realize she is not like her other peers (going through puberty with her peers). It could be a very difficult time for both of you as she strives to achieve her independence and still be like her friends. As I mentioned from personal experience earlier in chapter 2, it was an emotional time for me. Parents, please be sensitive and patient during this particular point in her life. I don't remember how long this stage lasted, but I'm sure it seemed like an eternity for my parents. One source of support I did not have in 1972 was being able to talk to other TS teens through e-mail, chatrooms, or even have the annual conference available to meet other families. I'm sure that would have helped immensely.

High School Age.

For me, these years did not seem as tumultuous as my preteen and junior high years. I hardly dated at all in high school, but I am pleasantly surprised to learn from talking to young TS women today—that dating is not as big of an issue as it used to be. Your self-image and self-esteem play a huge part in the social aspect of development. I still find this age group needs to be able to talk to others with TS their own age. I guess that's why the teen program is such a huge success at the TSSUS conferences. Things can get tough at times, which is why keeping the lines of communication open with your child is so important. Parents, don't feel bad if your daughter seems to be talking to her TS friends more than you. It is not only normal, but I would think it would be preferred to not talking at all. Giving your daughter respect and the space by letting her know you're always there for her will be a great comfort.

Adulthood.

I was making calls one time from our local chapter list, and I spoke to an adult TS woman who asked me to never call her again or send her anything in the mail with the words *Turner Syndrome* on it. I wondered, after I hung up, what kind of an environment she was raised in. I felt so sorry for her because it seemed she had no one and grew up actually ashamed of having TS. I can't imagine having that low of self-esteem. She would never be able to establish a real and loving relationship with anyone or any man until she loved herself first. Once you accept the fact that you have TS, you realize you are special not just because of that. You can be all that you can be when you reach a point of acceptance. You can then find contentment and complete fulfillment in adulthood. I'm not saying it that it's easy, but I'm looking forward to see how my daughter will face her future challenges and how it will mold her personality into adulthood. Hopefully, she will become a more independent, stronger, and confident woman.

CONCLUSION

I hope you enjoyed experiencing some insight into living with Turner Syndrome. This is my own personal journey, and I pray it has offered some sense of peace of mind to those who may be just newly diagnosed, or maybe you could even relate to my story if you are a TS woman reading this book. If you take only one thing away, it's to know that you are not alone when you get a TS diagnosis. There are so many resources out there and wonderful medical advances that are making TS girls or women's lives healthier and more positive. You are your best advocate, so don't be shy to ask for what you may need. The only way we are going to teach the public and medical community is to ask questions and educate them.

If you would like to learn more about research opportunities for TS and educational resources or locate your closest support group or chapter of the Turner Syndrome Society of the United States, please go to their website at www.turnersyndrome.org.

BIBLIOGRAPHY

Rieser, Patricia, CFNP, and Davenport, Marsha, MD, Turner Syndrome: A Guide for Families

Hamilton, Jill and Hozjan, Irena, *Turner Syndrome: Across the Lifespan*, The Turner Syndrome Society of Canada

INDEX

CPSIA information can be obtained
at www.ICGtesting.com
Printed in the USA
LVHW051452100619
620732LV00001B/41/P

9 781543 466096